Did She Rep

The Gentleman's Guide to Owning Online Dating (OkCupid & Match Edition)

By Patrick King

Dating and Image Coach at www.PatrickKingConsulting.com

Table of Contents

A quick note on captions.

Using the public opinion for your pictures [OkCupid]

Chapter Five: Optimization Workbook

The SURCCHH Questions

Chapter Six: Putting it all Together on OkCupid

SECTION ONE: MY SELF SUMMARY.

SECTION TWO: WHAT I'M DOING WITH MY LIFE.

SECTION THREE: I'M REALLY GOOD AT.

SECTION FOUR: THE FIRST THING PEOPLE NOTICE ABOUT ME.

SECTION FIVE: FAVORITE BOOKS, MOVIES, SHOWS, AND FOOD.

SECTION SIX: THE 6 THINGS I COULD NEVER DO WITHOUT.

SECTION SEVEN: I SPEND A LOT OF TIME THINKING ABOUT.

SECTION EIGHT: ON A TYPICAL FRIDAY NIGHT I AM.

SECTION NINE: THE MOST PRIVATE THING I'M WILLING TO ADMIT.

Introduction

Hello, and thanks for buying this book. My name is Patrick King, and I'm a dating and social skills coach. Unsurprisingly, these days much of my work pertains to how to adapt and take advantage of the new dating tech and human introduction systems that seem to be replacing many of our traditional methods. It's time to recognize, embrace, and own it.

Are you a fun-loving, laid-back, chill, and funny guy who loves traveling and hiking? Perhaps sarcasm is one of your greatest talents, and you are obsessed with Game of Thrones? Maybe you're the type of guy who loves to go out with friends, but also enjoys just staying in and watching Netflix? It is possible that you constantly think about food, or love photography and rock climbing? Hey, do you sometimes wish you had more time to meet people in real life? Are you looking for a relaxed person who makes you laugh?

Uh oh, did I just describe your profile in a nutshell? Fear not. Writing in remarkably undescriptive generalities is a common disease and I'm your Doctor Phil. I'll show you how to eliminate the boring from your entire online dating presence and *own* online dating all while being your genuine self. You'd ask an experienced friend when you should a text a woman or where to take her on a date. Why should things be different here? Let me show you how to hack, tweak, and optimize your online dating experience and get the most out of it.

This book is for anyone at any point on the spectrum, whether considering expanding your horizons by exploring online dating, or a grizzled online dating veteran looking to take their game to the next level.

My goals are simple: to teach you overwhelming success at online dating. For our purposes, this includes the following:

1. Creating an attractive, "complete package" online dating profile that attracts visitors, captures their attention, and makes her message *you*.

2. Writing messages that simply *beg* a response.

3. Converting online interactions into highly anticipated dates.

This whole process is entirely painless and can be done in minutes. You'll smack yourself in the face once you realize what you've been doing wrong, and just how easy it is to succeed. You'll (re)discover what makes you great. The immediate and future payoffs will be immense. You are literally pages away from all the dates you can handle from online dating.

Chapter One: Online Dating Analyzed

In this chapter, we'll examine the psychology behind online dating that sets the context for the methods in this book.

Let's get this out of the way immediately. There is absolutely NO stigma attached to online dating anymore. There are so many low-investment options such as Tinder, Down, and Coffee Meets Bagel that you'd be hard-pressed to find someone that hasn't dabbled in one of them.

So why do some people still refuse to try? The true reason is actually very simple: ego. Let's unpack this.

People naturally don't like rejection or failure. Not participating in something is a convenient excuse that allows them to avoid failure and preserve their self-esteem. Taking a proactive step simply opens you up to failure, where passivity leads to no possibility of failure. We see this in all other aspects of life, so it shouldn't be surprising to rear its ugly head in dating.

Example: Nah, I'm not going to try out for the basketball team. I'm too busy to practice every day. *No effort, convenient excuse, no rejection, self-esteem stays intact.*

Example: "Nah, I'm not going to talk to her. She's not cute." *No effort, convenient excuse, no rejection, self-esteem stays intact.*

Example: "Nah, I'm not going to do online dating. I'm not desperate." *No effort, convenient excuse, no rejection, self-esteem stays intact.*

See the parallels? We're not in high school anymore. It's okay to try.

So once you perform whatever mental gymnastics you need to overcome your ingrained beliefs, we arrive at a purely logical conclusion. To optimize your dating life, you need to meet as many women as possible and cast the widest net you can. Online dating is a natural and even necessary extension, because meeting people organically inevitably becomes too complicated, or simply slows to a trickle.

I also want to reiterate the point I made at the beginning of this chapter. The usage of online dating is through the roof, which means that people you know *will* see your profile. Embrace this, as you're being proactive and opening yourself up to vulnerability, which takes courage. And of course, you've seen their profile, so you're all in the same boat. It's like two men whose wives are friends who see each other in a gay strip club – there's an unspoken bond of understanding and to some degree of nondisclosure.

Now that we're ready to go full-steam ahead, we should explore a few unspoken truths of online dating.

Online Dating Truth One: You are a creep unless proven otherwise.

Safety and comfort are threshold issues for women. If they don't feel like they have those with you, say goodbye to any chance of meeting them in person.

This is a big reason why dating apps like Coffee Meets Bagel have been so successful. Women feel exponentially more comfortable using it because it matches you only with friends of friends on Facebook. The network effect creates an implicit level of trust and validation that automatically removes you from the creeper/stranger danger zone.

But for non-networked online dating, you are a complete stranger who may or may not be a crazy felon. You are not required to provide any identifying information such as your Facebook account or full name, so they may not be able to Google you to discover that you volunteer at a children's hospital weekly.

This means that your approach to women through online dating must combat this cautious approach, and engender feelings of safety and comfort. Overly aggressive online dating usually backfires, and you should err on the side of non-aggressiveness. Don't ask her to meet in an abandoned warehouse. You get the picture.

Online Dating Truth Two: Women are a hot commodity.

As someone who has created profiles for both genders, I know exactly what you're up against. Your average woman simply gets mobbed every day of the week. She will get in the neighborhood of 25-40 profile views, and 10-20 unsolicited messages a day. You can only imagine how it is for a highly desirable woman.

For the sake of comparison, a man is doing extremely well if he's getting 10 profile views a day, and 1 unsolicited message a day.

Can you imagine weeding out that many messages and profiles every day? They can't either – so they don't. They end up discarding messages for any possible pretext, sometimes without even realizing it. Here's a woman's train of thought when looking through her packed inbox:

1. Bad profile picture? Delete.

2. Blurry profile picture? Delete.

3. Typo in message or profile? Delete.

4. Bad joke? Delete.

5. Not into the same music/movies/hobbies? Delete.

6. Confusing or questionable username? Delete.

7. Generic profile? Delete.

This is why profile optimization is so important. Women have (somewhat justified) ADHD online, so you've got to stand out while avoiding that auto-delete pile.

Online Dating Truth Three: It's a numbers game.

Because of the pickiness that women are enabled with, online dating is a numbers game for even the most attractive men. Therefore, it's important to keep your expectations in line with reality.

Take OkCupid for example. OkCupid has repeatedly stated that the average reply rate for males hovers around 10-20%. A reply rate approaching 30-40% is considered to be doing very well, and a reply rate approaching 50% and above makes you a rockstar.

As a result, failure is inevitable even with highly-optimized profiles. Simply realize that these women are not actually judging *you*. They are judging your *profile and your ability to play the online game*, along with:

1. A sliver of your personality that, for whatever reason, didn't pique their curiosity.

2. Completely shallow and superficial factors (I once heard a lament, "He seemed cool, but he was only 5'10 and I like to date only 6' and taller.")

3. Reasons unrelated to you, such as the woman becoming serious with someone else.

4. Literally nothing. Through an account deactivation rate of 5-10%, and the sheer weight of their other messages and conversations, many women simply won't even get a chance to read your message.

We can optimize, tweak, and hack your profile and ability to play the game, but you'll still have to combat discouragement and adopt the mentality of conquering the percentages. Developing your ability to casually brush off rejection is half the battle to success at online dating.

Chapter Two: Getting the Right Start

In this chapter, we'll run through the initial setup for your profile, and other preliminary matters.

Curate your Internet presence

Though you are relatively anonymous with online dating, it's surprisingly easy to discover someone's identity with just their first name, city, and occupation. And you can bet your ass that you will be Googled. As a result, Google yourself and make sure you like what you see, including your social media profiles. Delete that tweet about getting trashed last night, and use nice pictures across the board.

OkCupid and Match are your best bets

This book is optimized for OkCupid and Match, and addresses specific functionality and questions you'll face on those sites (though the **SURCCHH** system, workbook, examples, and principles are fully transferrable to any dating site that allows you to write about yourself). 99% of the principles and system I teach are applicable to both OkCupid and

Match, and I make distinctions when appropriate, such as a separate Match chapter.

I'm a strong advocate of OkCupid and Match for a few reasons.

Match is paid, and as a result tends to have a much smaller user base than OkCupid. Most people assume that Match users are more serious about longterm dating and relationships than other sites, but this perception is actually false. If you use both sites, you'll see many of the same faces. However, for the age group of early 20s to mid 30s, it is the second most popular site, so it has the critical mass to find some quality matches.

OkCupid is free of course, which lowers the barrier and investment for anyone to join. This occasionally results in a lower quality of user, but as noted above, the userbase is not less serious about finding relationships than Match's. OkCupid is the most popular dating site for the early 20s to mid 30s age group, and has a user base that is relatively high quality, and that grows literally every single day.

I'm *not* a fan of Plenty of Fish. Even though it's free and boasts a very large user base, the average education and eligibility of the users tends to be lower. A hideous interface and functionality also make the site a chore to use.

Many other mobile-focused dating options have emerged, but none of them allow you to showcase your personality beyond 1-2 sentences. The effectiveness and efficiency of these options, (including Coffee Meets Bagel, How About We, Grindr, Tinder, Down, Skout, Blendr... the list goes on) can be difficult to compete with, but as long as people seek initial connections beyond a simple hookup, web-based online dating will always exist and even be preferable for some.

A winning username

Choosing a username should only take you a few minutes. Don't overthink it. The username is important, but its sole purpose is simply to get you in the door without setting off any alarms.

Word of caution – don't use your full name, or anything specific enough that it immediately leads to any other accounts you own and subsequently your identity when Googled. Don't let your efforts in creating a curated version of yourself go to waste! Finally, don't use nonsensical strings of letters or numbers.

Step 1: Write down specific aspects and traits about yourself. If you already have a username in mind, feel free to skip to step 3.

Example: My name is Jeff, I'm an engineer, I'm from Wisconsin, I like cooking, my favorite movie is Forrest Gump, I own a Labrador, and I like surfing.

Step 2: Think about how to combine these aspects, whether by humor, alliteration, non-sequiturs, inside jokes, or just good old-fashioned word mashing. I have 7 pieces of information from Jeff – see how many usernames I can brainstorm in 3 minutes. I came up with 13:

Example: jeffrunforrest, jeffjustcooks, dogownsjeff, jumpinjeff, landlockedsurfer, jeffnotgeoff, labnamedforrest, dogsurf, chefineer, surfchef, cookforrestcook, wisconsinsurf, UWbadgerjeff.

Step 3: Perform a sanity check. At first glance, is it confusing or too unusual? Think about what the first impression of the username is, and whether it is at all negative. If so, make it more generic. Is it masculine? Is it an inside joke? If so, would the average user understand the reference or be weirded out? And so on.

Chapter Three: The SURCCHH System

*In this chapter, I introduce the **SURCCHH** system and how you can apply it to your profile, messages, and daily life.*

The **SURCCHH** system (pronounced *"search"*) is the backbone of this book. In a medium where your entire identity is reduced to a picture and set of short answers, it is imperative to make a quick and lasting impression. Following **SURCCHH** and answering the **SURCCHH** questions is the guaranteed way to do that, and ingraining its meaning is the first step to optimizing your online profile.

SURCCHH defined

Specificity

If your profile is not specific, it is generic and boring. Don't use generalities. Use details – not mundane ones (you had wheat toast with strawberry jam at 10am this morning), but important clarifying and interesting ones. Detailed stories, traits, quirks, experiences, and descriptions are what make your profile noteworthy, and give women a sense of connection to you. Show, don't tell.

Example: I almost died last summer in Tibet at a temple, but a sherpa luckily had some crackers to calm the enraged goat. *As opposed to "I almost died in Tibet last summer."*

Example: I work at a charity that serves under-privileged kids every Sunday morning, and usually run the basketball and history classes. *As opposed to "I volunteer with kids occasionally."*

Uniqueness

This is similar to specificity, but worth an individual mention. Everyone has a unique aspect of their personality which makes them unlike anyone else – this is part of what the **SURCCHH** questions are designed to ferret out, so we'll address this later as well. Don't just stick with topics like traveling, eating at new restaurants, and what you studied in college. Once you identify your uniqueness, combine that with specificity.

Example: Since I was a kid, I've always wanted to hijack a fire hydrant for a pool party.

Example: I'm the world champion in the useless talents of eyebrow raising, and timing traffic lights.

Relatability

Guess why every election year we have presidential candidates giving talks in high-waisted jeans and tucked in polos? Why so much of stand-up comedy is simply an observation of behavioral patterns in daily life?

People like, and are drawn to, things that are familiar and similar to them.

This doesn't mean to try to mirror a woman's interests and say that you like all the same things, but to draw upon common experiences and descriptions that people are familiar with and understand. It builds a mental connection, makes you appear socially well-adjusted, and is often an easy humorous icebreaker. Get them nodding along, and make them think *"Hey, he's right, and that's funny!"* Bonus points if you create an observation that will make her think of you the next time she notices it in real life.

Example: I often find myself wondering what the proper etiquette is for walking into a row of seated people. Do I give them the butt or the crotch?

Example: Lately I've been on a documentary spree on Netflix, but I if I don't find something intriguing in the first 5 minutes, I just watch something I've already seen 10 times.

Confidence

While it's a thin line between bragging about your accomplishments and going overboard, you absolutely cannot come across as possessing low self-esteem. Confident guys make themselves vulnerable, aren't afraid to make fun of themselves, but will say what they want and perhaps brag a little. Avoid weak and insecure language, and hedging statements. *Note on vulnerability: it's great to be at terms with yourself and stay honest, but keep in mind which disclosures make for a good first impression, and which do not. You're selling yourself.*

One more perspective – projecting confidence is like that interview question "What's your greatest weakness?" Take any weakness you possess and turn it into a positive.

Example: I completely wiped out on the slopes this year, so my goal this winter is to master the bunny runs.

Example: I've been told that I'm a terrible navigator, but you'll be thanking me later for your extensive knowledge of the backroads of Chicago.

Calibration

Calibration is *you*. Learn the **SURCCHH** system, but don't feel compelled to abide by my examples and tone. You may not even agree with some of my principles, and that's fine. In order for you to be most effective, realize that you've got to make your profile a true extension of *you,* and highly calibrated to who you actually are. All we're doing here is drawing out the best parts of you and editorializing a bit.

Calibration affects how your profile reads, what you are doing in your profile photos, and most importantly, what kind of woman you will appeal to. No one can appeal to everyone, so there is something to be said for projecting who you are and owning that.

Example: I might be a little OCD about cleanliness of the dishes, bathroom, kitchen, carpet... let's just say I go through bottles of hand sanitizer in a month.

Example: This past summer was the third time I've been to the Minneapolis BDSM festival, and I'm happy to say this was the first year I was appropriately dressed. *Whoa, that escalated quickly.*

Humor

Sad fact of online dating: if you don't write with humor, you are automatically branded as boring. Your humor doesn't even have to be particularly funny, it just has to show that you're not a monotone and possess a sense of humor. Women see so many profiles that they need a reason to stay engaged and keep reading yours. And how many times have we heard that the number one trait that women are looking for is a sense of humor? But practice moderation, and be cautious of appearing like you are trying too hard. The majority of cocky humor has a high likelihood of backfiring without congruent body language and tone of voice, so beware.

Example: I asked around, and two words that kept coming up when my friends described me were loyal and enthusiastic. So... I'm basically a talking golden retriever?

Hooks

Each section, sentence, and message you write needs to contain a hook, which is an opening for a question, message, reply, or commonality. It's basically a statement that can be taken at face value, but also as the tip of an iceberg for people to inquire about. Many of these are subtle backdoor brags or humble brags, so they typically convey the message that you are high-value. This also means that you should examine whether your profile contains statements that are fluff and say nothing at all. Each statement should serve a purpose.

Example: Last summer, my annual surfing trip was ruined due to Hurricane Kate, but we befriended UFC fighters in the hotel bar.

Example: I love bringing back new cubicle decorations from every trip I take – my latest one is a Tibetan charm from Everest base camp.

Specificity, Uniqueness, Relatability, Confidence, Calibration, Humor, Hooks. Make sure to use them when writing anything for your online dating profiles, and you are guaranteed success.

Chapter Four: Your Photos

In this chapter, we'll go over how to optimize your photos, the most important part of your profile. Note: do __not__ upload pictures until your profile is entirely written and vetted. The reason is that you will be essentially invisible until your pictures are uploaded, so you should wait until your profile is 100% ready for viewing.

Unfortunately, the world we live in is a shallow one. The photo is *the* most important part of your profile. A great profile photo can redeem an otherwise lacking profile, and a bad profile photo can tank a great profile. This goes for every dating site out there, so it is crucial that you either find great pictures of yourself, or get a friend to take some.

I can't emphasize this last point enough – it's incredibly easy to get a haircut, grab a friend with a decent camera, grab a couple of different shirts, and head to a bar or park. You're putting in the effort in other areas of your profile, so why not take 20 minutes here?

How many?

I recommend that you have 4-5 pictures. I find that it's the perfect balance of showing yourself off without appearing vain. Any fewer and you can come off unsocial or insecure. This is also ideal because OkCupid shows three pictures when you hover over a user, so additional photos give women a reason to click to see more about you. Match automatically shows 5 total, 4 as thumbnails, so you should try to fill up that part of your profile.

Which should you use?

First of all, make sure they are high enough definition. No one wants to look at a fuzzy potato. Second, make sure you have good posture and body language. Third, make sure you are the focus of the picture, and it is easy to tell who you are. Fourth, rather than having 4-5 pictures of yourself in similar poses a la Derek Zoolander, I recommend choosing your pictures from the following categories:

1. Face and torso shot in which you are smiling. Make sure the resolution and size is adequate, because this will end up being your moneymaker picture. Make sure you are alone in this picture.

2. Action shot of you doing something interesting or in an interesting environment/setting, looking at the camera.

3. Action shot of you doing something interesting or in an interesting environment/setting, *not* looking at the camera.

4. An outdoorsy/activity shot. This is important to show that you are not at your computer all day long, even if you are.

5. A social shot where you are in a normal, social setting like a bar or a house with 1-3 other people.

6. Pictures that show humor.

7. Pictures with your pet or a cute animal. No overly feminine animals.

What pictures will make a woman roll her eyes?

Self-explanatory you'd think...

1. Blatant shirtless photos. This is somewhat contextual, as a picture of you surfing is much more acceptable than a shirtless selfie. But it's going to turn off 95% of women, while attracting 2%, so I usually recommend steering clear. If you've got a great body, there are many other

ways to show it off more subtly and without potential judgment. Why risk it?

2. Any type of selfie. This includes pictures from your webcam, laptop, and phone. Could you not find anyone else or any situation where photos were taken? It's tacky, and no one wants to see your dirty bathroom mirror.

3. Any picture with more than 3-5 people total, depending on the context. It's never good if I have to search for you in a picture, or am not sure which one you are. Girls will just be distracted and be likely to pass. Show that you have friends, but don't get lost within them.

4. Any group picture with other guys in which you are not clearly the most attractive person in the photo. Women often do this, and it almost always leads me to think *"Her friend is pretty cute... I wish I could message her instead."*

5. Highly-processed, edited, or filtered pictures. Instagram pictures on a case by case basis.

6. Duckfaces.

7. Pictures with props you don't know how to use. For example, motorcycles and guitars.

8. Pictures with a female that women might interpret to be an ex-girlfriend.

9. Pictures where you're frowning, look negative, or look emo.

10. Old pictures that you look nothing like anymore.

11. Pictures where you have sunglasses, or other objects obscuring your face.

As for your default thumbnail picture, I would use a photo from the face/torso category (of you alone!). The picture only shows up as a small thumbnail, so you have to make sure that there's a clear view of yourself. It's also extremely important because this is the picture that shows up in searches, as well as next to your messages.

A quick note on captions.

Captions are important. Keep your picture captions short. 1-2 sentences, and remember the **SURCCHH** system.

Example (hiking picture): Conquered: Mount Whitney. Next up: Mount Shasta.

Example (guy and dog): Me and my dog Dude – best marathon training buddy ever.

Example (face/upper body picture): Burning Man 2013 – right before the nudists descended on our camp.

Using the public opinion for your pictures [OkCupid]

First, you should consult female friends to help choose your photos with you.

After getting a feminine stamp of approval, OKC is generous enough to help you optimize your photos! It's at www.OkCupid.com/mybestface. It's a crowdsourced rating system, which lets the OKC community rate your pictures after you rate a certain amount of pictures for them.

Repeat this process until you have 4-5 photos that have been verified as optimal.

As a final thought, don't fall into the trap of linking your Instagram picture feed. You've worked carefully to create a curated and ideal version of yourself on your profile, so why potentially destroy that with your random Instagram food pictures?

Chapter Five: Optimization Workbook

In this chapter, we'll create the vast majority of the content for your profile and messages. Think hard!

"But there's nothing interesting about me, I'm boring." Absolutely untrue. Everyone has interesting experiences, thoughts, and stories that accumulate simply from living. Just because you don't travel to South America monthly or skydive with Richard Branson doesn't mean you don't have unique thoughts and experiences, even in your everyday life. We just have to delve into your life, draw them out to the surface, and portray them in the proper way.

Every **SURCCHH** question below is designed to elicit a **SURCCHH** system-approved statement for use in your profile. Notably, they are also designed to stay away from generic statements that other men often use. Put some good thought into this chapter, and it will provide you more than enough ammunition. It's likely that you've never thought of many of these questions, some might seem repetitive, and you might not even be able to answer some, but remember, your goal is to simply find the ones that resonate with you and capitalize. 1-2 of the statements you'll be creating contain so much more information and personality than you probably had in your entire profile.

And it's worth repeating that mini stories are the best. Notice how I'm not just answering the questions straight, but adding a bit of context, background, and description for each. Each answer should stand on its own, and not simply in direct response to the question itself. There is room for humor in most answers. Stay away from generalizations.

I recommend you write the answers on a separate document so you can draft, re-draft, ruminate, delete, edit, and have it all readily available for the following chapters. Aim to finish at least 15!

The SURCCHH Questions

1. What is your dream job? Silly and serious, though silly is often more usable.

Example: I have a huge sweet tooth, so I would love to be a modern-day Willy Wonka, minus the oompa loompa slave labor.

Example: I couldn't get enough of Indiana Jones as a kid, so I always dreamed of being a field archeologist digging for bones and lost relics.

2. How would you describe yourself as a child? And how does that relate to you as an adult? What would child you think of adult you?

Example: I was such a hyperactive child that I probably aged my parents more than the American presidency. As a result, my little brother got it super easy.

Example: When I was a kid, I knew that Santa was fake, but somehow believed that a rabbit delivered eggs filled with candy every Easter morning – I think I've retained my skill of selective belief.

3. What is your favorite quote, saying, or life motto? If it's generic like "Carpe Diem," don't bother, or think of a less generic way to say it. Sincerity works.

Example: I forget the source, but for each major decision in my life, I try to keep the following in mind: "There are always a million reasons to not do something."

4. What is the most interesting thing you did in the past month? Doesn't have to be inherently interesting, just something you can talk about or create a good story around.

Example: A couple weekends ago, I partook in the most intense game of Cards Against Humanity + Jenga north of the border. I love how it brings a dark side out in people.

Example: I recently sang at a friend's wedding, and didn't receive a compliment from anyone under age 60. I might be doing something wrong... or very right.

5. What is the most worthwhile and satisfying thing you've done in the past 5 years? Be sincere.

Example: Though it seems like everyone's got a DSLR these days, I'm incredibly grateful that I picked up photography a few years ago. I love the ability to return to little moments even years later.

Example: My favorite work-related memories are from when I was a dietician a few years ago. It was so great to see people's self-esteem gradually rise as they became healthier and looked better.

6. What's the weirdest/funniest situation you've ever faced in the city you currently reside in?

Example: The last time I walked into the south part of town, I nearly got drawn into an argument between a monk and a skinhead (not Halloween). Not my best Friday night.

Example: My last night out: White Russians, screaming Italian grandmothers, churros, and the world's smelliest hobo. Boston, never change.

7. What is your favorite spot in the city you currently reside in, and the world in general? Sincerity can work.

Example: My favorite spot in the city is Outlook Grove – my parents used to take me there when I was young, and I still bike there from time to time to unwind after work.

Example: I can't wait for the day when I accrue enough PTO to return to Gibraltar. Talk about feeling insignificant!

8. Is there a cool advancement in your field/profession that you can geek out about in general terms? Make sure people outside of your field would actually care.

Example: I'm a lawyer, and you would be justified if your eyes glazed over just then, but I've been enjoying being the sounding board for my friends for things like Prop 8 and this whole NSA thing!

Example: I love being in biology because we're just beginning to figure out how to personalize medicine and treatment to our individual bodies. Definitely has a GATTACA feel to it, but in a good, non-eugenics way.

9. What 2 useless talents do you possess? Shoot for funny and random ones.

Example: Not to brag... but when I was 8, I had the best show and tell of the day for doing a headstand and finishing a can of soda through a straw. I'm also a bona fide award-winning pumpkin carver.

10. What 3 real talents do you possess?

Example: I've been told that I'm a pretty good cook, but it's just something that relaxes me so it's a win-win. However, messing up a beef wellington is NOT relaxing.

11. What part of your daily routine or part of your day is unique?

Example: Every morning, I kickstart my day by brushing my teeth for as long it takes me to check my email. Thankfully I get enough email on weekends as well.

Example: I really wish I didn't sit so close to the bathroom at work because I pretty much know everyone's pee schedule at this point.

12. What are 3 big pet peeves you have? Shoot for common and funny ones.

Example: I hate it when you wave at someone, but they were actually waving at someone behind you? I've mastered the "Oh, nope, just stroking my hair" move.

13. What's your favorite animal and why?

Example: I've always liked wolverines. Aside from the X-Man, they're cute and cuddly, but punch way above their weight class.

14. What music do you shamelessly rock out to?

Example: I may or may not have an entire playlist dedicated to Michael Bolton and other singer-instrumentalists.

15. What would you be doing if you were wealthy enough to not have to work? Alternatively, an interesting retirement plan?

Example: If I won the lottery tomorrow, I think I might open a high-end barbershop. From my experience, it just involves hanging out with people with aprons on.

16. What does your dream house contain?

Example: A pre-requisite of mine when I was moving was proximity to public transport, but one day a prerequisite will be whether or not there is a gym in the house and a wooden porch I can fix up.

17. Name 3 random thoughts you often have in public.

Example: Sometimes when I walk down the street, I can't help but wonder how many people are just thinking about their next meal.

18. What are your 4 main interests that are not work-related? This is a good place to explain a couple of passions of yours. Sincerity works best.

Example: I played in a band when I was younger, and though I only pick up my guitar once in a blue moon now, I consider music to be a large part of my identity.

19. Name 4 hobbies and 2 unique things that have happened while doing each of them. Convey a sense of passion and ambition.

Example: Like all Asians, I did kung fu when I was younger, and I have it to thank for the most hardcore injury of my life: a broken toe.

20. What is a funny thing that your hometown is known for (can be made up)?

Example: I'm from a small town in Pennsylvania, and we played hide and seek in gigantic cornfields as kids – in hindsight this seems like a terrible and alarming idea.

21. Why did you go into your current career path, and where do you hope it will lead to? Or just talk about what you do for a living. Convey a sense of ambition and passion.

Example: I'm a product manager at a good-sized photo technology startup. It's not quite where I thought I would be after studying philosophy in college, but I'm learning as much as possible to apply to my own upcoming ventures.

22. How would you describe your current phase of life and why you're online dating, or dating in general? Sincere.

Example: After coming to a new job with less crazy hours, I've decided to allow my friends to finally peer pressure me into online dating.

23. Has a book, song, piece of art, or anything else provoked you into deep thought or affected you otherwise? Sincere.

Example: Seeing the Hiroshima Peace Plaza in Japan was one of the most simultaneously uplifting and depressing days ever.

24. What are 3 things you do that no one else probably does?

Example: I think I've definitely got the first rights to a patent on a methodology for optimal cleanliness in wiping down my bathroom and kitchen counters.

25. What are 3 adjectives you would use to describe yourself? Take this opportunity to reflect on how you want yourself to come across and be perceived in general.

Example: I like to think of myself as charming in a bring-home-to-grandma sense, doubly so if she's a sassy old broad.

26. What are 2 examples or stories of each of those adjectives?

Example: I've been known to get unreasonably competitive during Cranium – the last time the box came out, it didn't close until 3am.

27. What 2 adjectives would your best friends use to describe you? Sincere works here.

Example: In the past, my friends have described me as the one they go to for honesty – they know that I'm always looking out for them and don't just tell them what they want to hear.

28. What is a funny quirk about your body that you would have to tell someone borrowing it?

Example: You might not notice it about me on first glance, but my back cracks are the second loudest noise I can make.

Example: I swam competitively as a kid, but that's my least favorite sport now because my ears don't take kindly to chlorinated water anymore.

29. Who is your favorite fictional character? Humor is better here.

Example: I wish I was Harvey Specter.

Example: My role model is Robert Downey Jr.'s Ironman, minus the goatee because I can't grow it.

30. Are there any fictional or historical characters that you especially identify with? Who and why? This can be serious or funny.

Example: I couldn't watch "Old School" without harking back to my fraternity days – we even had our own Blue! He did survive the pledging period, however.

31. What was the best purchase of your life, cheap or expensive? Sincere or funny.

Example: The best purchase of my life was my cheapo Craigslist roadbike. There's no better way to get around the city, and I'm slowly becoming an obnoxious hip biker.

32. Have you had a brush with a celebrity, or 15 minutes of fame otherwise?

Example: For you Breaking Bad fans, I once shouted "Yo, bitch!" at Aaron Paul and he turned around and gave me a middle finger.

33. What are 2 questions you have always wondered about the world, life, and universe? Sincere.

Example: Sometimes when I have trouble sleeping at night, my mind starts thinking through the steps I would need to take to drop everything, move, and become a farmer. There's a spreadsheet floating around on my computer somewhere I wrote in a haze one night.

34. What is something simultaneously embarrassing and funny about yourself?

Example: I have the weakest stomach if I'm not driving or steering – I've gotten motion sick on boats, bars, buses, canoes, rowboats, rollercoasters, you name it.

35. Are there any funny awards that you have won for something completely inconsequential? You can feel free to make up something silly to showcase a talent.

Example: I once won a karaoke competition with "Bad Romance" by Lady Gaga. Costumes and dancing were involved.

36. Have you ever been part of, or a victim of a particularly good prank?

Example: I think I deserve an award for this prank: when a roommate was gone for 3 weeks and told us not to go inside his room, we took a series of themed photos in there and sent them to him – Hawaiian, robot, and Twilight themes included.

37. What is something you thought was lame until you tried it?

Example: I was one of those suckers that actually obeyed the instructions on the q-tip box to not go inside the ear canal... until about 4 years ago. Life. Changing.

Example: I shamelessly wear my Crocs if I know I'm going to be walking for a long period of time.

38. What's the best or most useful life tip you've learned in the past couple of years? Or in your life?

Example: My key to productivity is that this past year I learned the Seinfeld method of productivity (bear with me): buy one of those big wall calendars, and put a big X through each day that you've accomplished what you wanted. After a few days, your only job is to keep the chain unbroken.

39. What item in your room would require the funniest explanation?

Example: I actually own one of the original helmets from the Power Rangers TV show, a practical joke by my friends gone awry... and awesome. Go red!

40. What is your Meyers-Briggs personality type (women will probably know theirs)?

Example: For those that read into it, I'm an ENFP.

41. What are 2 examples of funny awkwardness that has happened to you from the past 5 years?

Example: Sometimes I think I'm relatively normal, but then other times I walk into a pole while talking to someone and have to get stitches.

42. Do you have a good, short story about your username?

Example: As for my username: I'm from the country's cheese capital, but I somehow developed a taste for the beach and surfing... suffice it to say, I don't visit home too often. *(for landlockedsurfer)*

43. Do you daydream much? What about?

Example: When I have downtime at work, I'm doing one of two things – slyly arranging my screen to make it look like reddit is a word document, or daydreaming about what dogs think when they stick their heads outside of car windows.

44. What embarrassing and funny story would your friends tell about you?

Example: If you meet my friends, they'll do their best to embarrass me by telling the story of when I broke my foot kicking a piece of concrete that looked like a ball. Pre-empted! Besides, my purple cast was the envy of all.

45. What new product or service would you be first in line to try?

Example: I would be the first sign-up, purchaser, and reviewer if anyone could ever come up with a caffeine intake system that tells you exactly how long you'd be wired for.

46. What old and revived product/service/anything do you miss and want to come back?

Example: Whatever happened to the Animaniacs? I'd watch the crap out of it if it was ever revived. If a petition doesn't exist, I'm going to start it tomorrow.

47. What are you looking forward to in the near or distant future?

Example: I'm counting down the days until the Wolfpack plays the Wolverines. Go Nevada!

48. What is a family tradition that shows how close you are to your family? If not tradition, then story or memory. Sincere.

Example: I love Decembers for the weather, and going with my family to cut down our annual Christmas tree. My kids will never have an artificial tree.

49. Do you have a pet? Funny story, cute story, or sincere feelings.

Example: My best friend besides my dad is my 11-year dog Bub. Last year I bought an old baby stroller so he can still go on our morning walks in the park.

50. Is there anything else notable about yourself that you want to list?

At this point, you should feel that just about every essential aspect of yourself, and interesting experience/thought is listed here – you will basically have your identity written out, in **SURCCHH** system-approved terms no less! And if you notice that some important aspect of yourself is missing, now you know what it is. Through this method, you've clearly showcased your personality, and moved beyond a simple list of adjectives.

Chapter Six: Putting it all Together on OkCupid

In this chapter, you will put it all together: take the raw materials you created in the previous workbook chapter and mold them to the OKC profile. Remember, be sure to not upload your profile photos until you've perfected the content. I also recommend not typing directly into the OKC fields. Rather, open up a Word document so you can upload it all simultaneously, and run spelling and grammar checks multiple times.

By the time any woman reads your profile, she is intrigued enough by either your picture or your message to have clicked on it. Whichever the case, the profile must do the following: increase the intrigue, entice her to message you or reply to your message, and not mess up the momentum you already have. You're selling yourself, so put your best foot forward!

Editorialize a little, but don't lie.

Example: If you're the office's IT guy, you *actually* run the technology department and are the resident problem solver.

Example: If you occasionally volunteer at a convalescent home, you *actually* love working with older folks on a regular basis because they remind you of your own grandparents, and are the best listeners.

See how much better the second ones sound?

Other general tips on taking your answers from the **SURCCHH** questions and translating them into your profile:

1. Don't give her any reasons to say no, while giving her as many reasons to say yes.

2. *NO verbal diarrhea.* Don't be long-winded, and cut the clutter. Don't ask rhetorical questions and converse with yourself. A wall of text is synonymous with a few things, including self-absorption, eyes glazing over, and boringness. And we all know what any of those lead to – delete! The examples in this chapter add up to a profile that is between 600-700 words. Use that as a guideline.

3. Avoid statements that don't actually say anything. Each sentence should have a point and add to your attraction.

4. Don't just answer the question directly and leave it at that. Remember how my **SURCCHH** question answers were mini stories and stood on their own?

5. Don't fall in love with the way you've written sections so much that it would prevent you from re-writing them better.

6. <u>READ IT OUT LOUD AND CHECK YOUR SPELLING AND GRAMMAR!</u>

One final reminder of what our overarching goal is here: we're not trying to paint a comprehensive picture of ourselves. We're just demonstrating our personalities and traits in a positive and charming light.

SECTION ONE: MY SELF SUMMARY.

This is the first section at the top of the page, so it needs to pop and make you stand out immediately. Make sure you include at least some substantive information about yourself – try to shoot for a 2-3 more serious and sincere workbook answers, and 2-3 less serious ones. This is a good rule of thumb for each subsequent section.

People often make the mistake of listing a bunch of adjectives about themselves – don't fall into this temptation! It's a violation of **SURCCHH**, and most of those adjectives apply to most people anyway, so it's like you've said nothing about yourself. Remember, we're showing your personality and traits through stories and imagery that you've generated from the **SURCCHH** questions.

Generic alert (no-nos):

1. "I'm a transplant."

2. "I'm shy until you get to know me."

3. "I don't like to talk about myself, so just ask me for more info/find out in person."

4. "I love to travel." *I'm sure you do, but I'm willing to bet that this phrase appears in 99% of profiles. So either don't put it, or distinguish yourself from every other guy who says this. Don't just use travel as a proxy for being adventurous and interesting, you're so much more than that!*

5. "I hate/am horrible at writing things like this."

6. "I hate drama."

7. "I'm searching for my partner in crime."

8. "I'm tired of meeting people in the bar/club scene."

9. "Sometimes I'm x, other times I'm opposite of x."

10. "I love to laugh and have fun." *Who doesn't?*

11. "I'm laidback, easy-going, and like to have fun."

12. Explaining that you're on the site because work leaves you with little time otherwise.

13. Using the word "wanderlust."

Sample templates (Workbook question numbers. Note that you don't have to stay in the order listed):

1. 3, 8, 15, 20

2. 1, 7, 26, 40, 42

3. 2, 14, 27, 30

4. 6, 16, 29, 32, 43

5. 4, 5, 9, 18, 42

Sample template 1 (3, 8, 15, 20):

Geek alert: I'm an astronomer and a Star Trek fanatic, and the latter actually inspired the former. The first thing I do each morning is check the news to see what new planets we've discovered that are capable of sustaining life. Told you!

I love what I do, but if I ever struck it big and could hang up the ol' telescope, I'd ideally buy an island retreat/evil lair a la Richard Branson and privately finance my own space missions. That, and a lot of rock climbing and surfing.

I'm from a small town in Virginia best known for our liberal use of butter in every dish and drink. It's like Paula Deen's spirit resides here, I swear. Some of my older relatives have tried to sneak butter into my orange juice while I wasn't looking. Despite this, my entire extended family is one of my top priorities in life, and I can't wait to go home every holiday season.

I'm generally not big on poetry, but the mantra that keeps me hustling on a daily basis is Robert Frost's "The Road Not Taken." It's guided a majority of my major life decisions since high school.

SECTION TWO: WHAT I'M DOING WITH MY LIFE.

Discuss your profession, life goals, intramural sports teams, and current volunteer activities – things of that nature. *What fills your days?* Don't dwell on school or your job because they do not define you as a whole. As with before, include some substantive information, and choose 1-2 more serious answers from your workbook answers, and 1-2 more humorous answers. Finally, don't be repetitive with the above My Self Summary section.

Generic alert:

1. "I'm a ___ by day, and a ___ by night."

2. "Writing this profile."

3. "Living it."

4. "Figuring it out."

Sample templates (Workbook question numbers):

1. 4, 8

2. 21, 32

3. 21, 41

4. 6, 22

5. 8, 10

Sample template 2 (21, 32):

I'm currently a manager at a securities firm – thank you, undergrad economics degree. I somehow imagined there would be more "Wall Street" type situations, but I can tell you that among managing some pretty sizeable clients, I'm also a wizard with Excel now.

I play basketball a couple days a week, and on weekends I'm usually trying to recapture the glory that was an awkward photo-bombing by Jonah Hill circa 2010. I also recently picked up the cello, which provides the greatest joys and frustrations of my everyday life.

SECTION THREE: I'M REALLY GOOD AT.

In my opinion, this isn't where you truly brag. You can do one of the following things:

1. Brag about real talents in a funny, maybe even self-deprecating way.
2. Brag about fun and stupid talents in a genuine way.

3. Brag about real talents in a genuine way... but only if actually *objectively* really cool and unique.

Anything else, in my experience, and you risk activating the arrogance alert. Outright bragging is tough to do correctly without congruent body language and tone of voice. As with before, 1-2 more serious answers, or 1-2 sillier answers, or a mixture of the two.

The most generic answer here is sarcasm.

Sample templates (Workbook question numbers):

1. 9, 24
2. 10, 28
3. 9, 35
4. 14, 43
5. 24, 38

Sample template 1 (9, 24):

In first grade I was crowned the multiplication tables king of the entire grade... but I was unseated by the kid who always had his shoes untied.

I'm also probably the best in the world at isolating the crunchiest fallen leaves and crushing them under my foot.

SECTION FOUR: THE FIRST THING PEOPLE NOTICE ABOUT ME.

This section is very simple, and I find that there aren't that many ways to approach it. Notably, the best answers to this *aren't* about your visual appearance. You can:

1. Answer truthfully if you truly have something unique.

2. Make something up funny about your personality, physical appearance, or mannerisms.

3. Brag about a funny talent, or something silly.

Don't outright brag, unless it's something you're very sure about and can do it in a subtle way.

Generic alert:

1. "I don't know, you tell me!"
2. "My eyes."

Sample templates (Workbook question numbers):

1. 28
2. 24
3. 9
4. 34
5. 41

Sample template 3:

If music is at all appropriate, and someone made the mistake of trusting me to DJ, I can make a 90's hip-hop playlist that will kickstart any party, guaranteed.

SECTION FIVE: FAVORITE BOOKS, MOVIES, SHOWS, AND FOOD.

Limit yourself to 3-5 of each. Remember **SURCCHH** here in particular – don't put things that everyone else does. Most people don't read this section very

carefully, and even gloss over it unless they truly feel strongly about a music artist or movie, etc. Just list 3-5 of each, with an extra sentence either describing your general taste, or commenting about one of the things you put. Finally, don't format this with bullet points, because it will make the section look way too long.
Tip: for food, you can easily put well-known dishes or restaurants in your town to use in messages later.

Cautionary examples:

1. "Harry Potter, Hunger Games, The Great Gatsby"

This just makes me think that you only read these because movies exist.

2. "Of Mice and Men, Huckleberry Finn, 1984"

This just makes me think you don't read at all, because these are all high school curriculum books.

3. "I listen to everything but country and rap."

No one likes everything, and it's off-putting to hate on things. It's also so broad and vague that you might as well not have put anything.

4. "I love all food except ____."

Same comment as #3.

Sample section 5:

Books: Truthfully, I don't have the time to read many full novels, but the ones I do are mostly motivational and entrepreneurship books like So Good They Can't Say No, and the Four Hour Work Week.

Movies: Superbad (I met Michael Cera in person once – turns out that his awkward "acting" really is just him), Back to the Future, 300

Shows: Parks and Rec, Sleepy Hollow, Breaking Bad, and various trashy reality shows – they are fantastic for entertainment value per minute.

Music: Lately I've been on a jazz kick with lots of Joe Pass and Coltrane, but vintage Miles Davis is my all-time favorite.

Food: I'll keep this simple – Glenlivet on the rocks, pineapple fried rice (from Thai King on 3rd Street), a glazed donut, and lasagna.

SECTION SIX: THE 6 THINGS I COULD NEVER DO WITHOUT.

SURCCHH is especially important here as well, because there are a lot of possible generic answers. Simply list 6 things/people/concepts/places that have some meaning to you – maybe with a hook involved. They don't have to be inherently unique. If you want to mix it up, you can do a list of other things, such as "6 things I hate," "6 things I am mildly attached to," "The last 6 things I bought on Amazon," ""The 6 things I use most in my daily life," or "6 things I keep meaning to buy." If you stray from the original prompt here, it *must* be funny.

Generic alert:

1. "Phone, internet, air, food, water, friends, family, laughter, sunshine, meaningful relationships, passion, etc" *In other words, don't answer this question literally.*

Sample section 6:

I thought a more entertaining list might be 6 things that I keep meaning to buy, so here goes: walkie talkies, post-its, quality headphones (any suggestions?), new socks, a French press, and biking gloves.

SECTION SEVEN: I SPEND A LOT OF TIME THINKING ABOUT.

You get a free pass to be silly on this one. I suspect that was the original intent of this question – to allow users to show some personality and silliness if they haven't already. It's fine to keep this short, simple, random, and funny. You can also lean towards philosophical and deep, if you wish. This is a good section for hooks, because they could be questions that you pose.

Generic alert:

1. "My next meal."
2. "Where I'm traveling to next."

Sample templates (Workbook question numbers):

1. 17
2. 33
3. 43
4. 47
5. 8

Sample template 1 (silly):

I wonder how long that dog has been tied up outside that café? Is the owner watching? Can I rescue him? Interspersed with: where is the best burrito in Minneapolis?

Sample temple 3 (philosophical):

Sometimes I catch myself thinking about the lives of my co-workers, and how even though our lives are intersecting now, how far we'll diverge in a couple of years.

SECTION EIGHT: ON A TYPICAL FRIDAY NIGHT I AM.

Here's the thing about this section: it's not actually about what you do on a typical Friday night. Do not answer this literally. Instead, rephrase to this: "What would a fun night/date with me look like?" I find it's best to just list a couple of specific, fun activities here. Keep in mind that there are two main avenues: you can either focus on alcohol, or activities, so pick whichever is more calibrated towards you personally.

Generic alert:

1. "There's no typical Friday night for me."

2. "Out with my friends."

3. "Either out with my friends, or relaxing at home." *Duh.*

4. Mentioning Netflix.

Sample section 8:

Alcohol: A couple of snakebites at MX bar, maybe followed by karaoke in Japantown, topped off by people watching while grooving to electronic music.

Activities: Checking out the newest urban art installations, then binging on fast food while Yelping where the nearest jazz show is.

SECTION NINE: THE MOST PRIVATE THING I'M WILLING TO ADMIT.

It probably needs to be said – please don't actually admit anything very private, like your rap sheet or what's under your bed.

Instead, this is kind of a free section to either brag in a stupid/funny way (like **SURCCHH** questions 1, 9, 19,

32, 37), go on a complete non-sequitur, or say something embarrassing and endearing.

Generic alert:

1. "Ask me."
2. "Then it wouldn't be private!"
3. "That I'm on OkCupid."
4. "I'm not going to say that here."
5. "You'll have to find out in person."

Sample section 9:

Embarrassing/funny: I was totally a fat kid growing up. Those fruit roll ups will get you.

Stupid/funny brag: I own a sewing machine and have made my own blankets. Renaissance man.

Non-sequitur: My dream job is to be Anthony Bourdain's sidekick that he doesn't like very much: very little screen time and work, but I still get to party all over the world.

SECTION TEN: YOU SHOULD MESSAGE ME IF…

If you don't have any hard deal breakers (and let's be honest, you probably don't), you should just leave this section blank. As a guy, you won't be depending on incoming messages, and very little in this section actually makes a difference as to who messages you or not. There are just too many ways to backfire here and appear close-minded, picky, unreasonable, or even too open. If you feel strongly about it, fill it out truthfully and sincerely, but be aware that it's too easy to come off negatively here. Remember, don't use statements that say essentially nothing like "I want someone nice, fun, honest, and funny."

Sample section 10:

I'm looking for someone that cracks me up and sometimes thinks I am funny as well. Bonus if you've ever been referred to as "sassy" or "outrageous."

SECTION ELEVEN: MY DETAILS (THE SIDEBAR).

Be truthful, but here are a few thoughts to consider:

1. Don't put your income. It's a trap, and you lose either way.

2. Don't lie about your height. 1 inch tops. TOPS.

3. Don't oversell or undersell your body type. Basically, don't appear arrogant, and don't appear unconfident.

4. Don't fill in the drugs question.

5. If you are religious and actually care, note it. Religion or lack thereof is a very common auto-delete factor, and it will increase your chances with women of your religion exponentially.

6. Don't tick off that "Casual Sex" box, even if it is truthful. This is going to be a huge red flag for 99% of women, while appealing to 1%. The odds just don't make sense for you to be truthful.

Chapter Seven: Putting it all together on Match

Now that we've got our system, principles, and context from the OkCupid chapter (if you didn't read that chapter, go back and do it now!), I'll introduce my thoughts on each Match profile section and how you should approach it. The biggest, if only difference in how to write for Match as opposed to OkCupid, is that you must be much more brief because of the character limit. This is a double-edged sword.

Thankfully, the Match questions are either too general or too specific for there to be many generic alerts, but the ones listed for OkCupid are still valid. Headlines are a different matter...

HEADLINE

The headline usually stops people dead in their tracks. How do you find something that encompasses yourself in just one sentence? Well, you can't... so don't make that your goal.

Just remember what we're doing with everything else in this book: abiding by **SURCCHH**, and not giving women a reason to say no. There are so many approaches here that there isn't much else to talk about, so let's get on to the templates and examples.

Remember, the headline isn't supposed to really describe your entire being in one sentence. It's just something to grab attention and not make women run away. There is only one ironclad rule: it must be funny.

Generic alert:

1. Hi.

2. Live, love, laugh.

3. Looking for Ms. Right/my partner in crime.

4. Not sure what to put here.

5. I can't believe I'm online dating.

6. Does anyone actually read these?

7. Insert funny headline here.

SURCCHH answers to use: 1, 6, 7, 9, 13, 14, 17, 18, 19, 20, 27, 28, 29, 32, 37, 43, 44, 49.

Sample 1: Wanted: Willy Wonka's job.

Sample 16: You're not reading this, you're planning your next meal.

Sample 14: Powered by Michael Bolton playlists.

Sample 32: Once cursed at Aaron Paul.

Sample 37: Shamelessly wears Crocs.

You get the idea.

FOR FUN

This is a combination of the following OkCupid questions:

1. My Self Summary
2. What I'm Doing With My Life
3. I'm Really Good At
4. On A Typical Friday Night I Am

This is extremely open-ended, as Match questions sometimes are. (On a digression, this is a mistake on Match's part, because while it allows for a far wider range of answers, it's ultimately too flexible to be filled out easily. Such questions just breed analysis paralysis, while more pointed questions are more easily answered and used.) As with OkCupid questions, I suggest using 1-2 humorous answers, along 1-2 more sincere answers. This is the place to talk about your hobbies interests, and passions, not work. What do you do off-hours, or what would you like to do? **SURCCHH** dictates that you not just state your preference for mountain climbing and running.

Sample templates:

1. 4, 5, 20

2. 44, 38, 32

3. 7, 9, 17

4. 4, 26, 31

Sample template 1:

Last weekend, I partook in the most intense game of Cards Against Humanity + Jenga seen north of the border. When not being competitive, I take as many pictures as possible with my new DSLR. Thankfully, I don't play hide and seek in giant cornfields anymore like I did as a kid.

MY JOB

This is one of Match's only straightforward and direct questions. This is pretty much the same as the OkCupid question What I'm Doing With My Life but with only the professional aspect.

Talk about your job, how you ended up there, your passion for it, and your professional and personal ambitions and aspirations. Don't go into too much detail, especially industry-specific detail, because no one will care. Do not be negative about your job, because that will make you sound bitter and unfulfilled in life. Talk about the circumstances about how your life intertwines with your job, and the emotions that feelings you have from that, not just a one sentence answer like "I'm a programmer at an early stage company."

Sample templates:

1. 8

2. 21

3. 44

4. 1

Sample template 2:

I'm currently a manager at a securities firm — thank you, undergrad economics degree. I somehow imagined there would be more "Wall Street" type situations, but I can tell you that among managing some pretty sizeable clients, I'm also a wizard with Excel now.

MY RELIGION

There aren't many approaches to this question, and honestly, there shouldn't be. Religion is (justifiably) a dealbreaker, so you should be honest about your religious preferences and participation. However, as with all things, don't be too extreme or too detailed. Keep it light if you can and don't disrespect others here.

Sample: I'm a Christian. I wouldn't say that I'm extremely observant, as church is more of an Easter, Christmas, and the occasional Sunday affair.

FAVORITE HOT SPOTS

This is essentially the same as the OkCupid question of On a Typical Friday Night I Am. There's no need for me to talk much more about it here, other than the fact that you can and should include daytime activities and locales here as well.

Sample: Checking out the newest urban art installations, then binging on fast food while Yelping where the nearest jazz show is.

FAVORITE THINGS

Another Match question that is essentially the same as an OkCupid question. In the OkCupid question, you were limited to food, books, movies, and TV. You get a little more freedom here, but there is much less space. Here are some suggested ways to go if you want to branch out a bit: location, vacation spot, type of coffee, time of day, part of your daily life, type of animal, expression/saying, sports teams, etc. The list goes on, but notice that I did not list video games.

Sample:

Movies: Superbad, Back to the Future, 300

TV: Parks and Rec, Sleepy Hollow, and Breaking Bad

Music: Lately I've been on a jazz kick with lots of Joe Pass and Coltrane, but vintage Miles Davis is my all-time favorite.

I also live for donuts, pineapple fried rice, and whiskey.

LAST READ

Though worded differently, I would encourage you to treat this essentially the same as the OkCupid question about favorites. Here's the rub: very few people actually read much on a regular basis. So what do you do when the last book you read was 50 Shades of Grey, or from 2 years ago? I recommend that you simply reach 5 years back into your reading history and pick 3-5 books after make sure they aren't weird or super generic. Abide by **SURCCHH** here, and don't simply answer this question with 1 sentence. Don't admit that you don't read at all.

Sample:

The last books I read and really enjoyed are all entrepreneurial and motivational in nature: 4 Hour Work Week, Never Eat Alone, Crossing the Chasm. One day I'll begin the Game of Thrones series...

ABOUT ME AND WHAT I'M LOOKING FOR

This is a combination of essentially every OkCupid question, especially:

1. My Self Summary

2. Message Me If...

Since there's no character limit here, I recommend using as much space as you can. Therefore, I would go with 2-3 humorous answers and 2-3 serious answers. Take advantage of the space given to make yourself stand out here!

I recommend focusing on details about yourself and not your future partner for two reasons. First, as I've stated before, it's unlikely that you have any real dealbreakers, so don't take the risk of looking picky or closeminded. Second, if you write something generic like "I'm just looking for someone that's kind, sweet, and has a great sense of humor," well, that's just fluff and violates **SURCCHH**. Everyone wants that.

So basically, write a self summary like the OkCupid guidelines give, then add a sentence about something specific or funny you're looking for.

Sample templates (Workbook question numbers. Note that you don't have to stay in the order listed):

6. 3, 8, 15, 20

7. 1, 7, 26, 40, 42

8. 2, 14, 27, 30

9. 6, 16, 29, 32, 43

10. 4, 5, 9, 18, 42

Sample template 1 (3, 8, 15, 20):

Geek alert: I'm an astronomer and a Star Trek fanatic, and the latter actually inspired the former. The first thing I do each morning is check the news to see what new planets we've discovered that are capable of sustaining life. Told you!

I love what I do, but if I ever struck it big and could hang up the ol' telescope, I'd ideally buy an island retreat/evil lair a la Richard Branson and privately finance my own space missions. That, and a lot of rock climbing and surfing.

I'm from a small town in Virginia best known for our liberal use of butter in every dish and drink. It's like Paula Deen's spirit resides here, I swear. Some of my older relatives have tried to sneak butter into my orange juice while I wasn't looking. Despite this, my entire extended family is one of my top priorities in life, and I can't wait to go home every holiday season.

I'm generally not big on poetry, but the mantra that keeps me hustling on a daily basis is Robert Frost's "The Road Not Taken." It's guided a majority of my major life decisions since high school.

I'd love to find someone that embodies the word active, and doesn't mind the occasional dance battle.

WINKING

I don't think you should use the wink feature at all. It tells the other user that you find them attractive, and basically puts the onus on them to initiate the conversation. By this point, we know that women are very rarely going to initiate conversations because of their overactive inboxes. Additionally, it has the side effect of making you appear lazy, passive, and somewhat afraid of messaging them. That's not what women want in general, and that's a death knell in online dating when women are inundated with messages as they are. A strong message is a better move 100% of the time.

Chapter Eight: Gaming the System [OkCupid]

In this chapter, we talk about using facets of OKC's system to optimize your exposure on the site.

Now that you have a great profile, we have to ensure that it is actually viewed by women. When you first make your profile you'll show up far higher in searches and on sidebars that show users. However, people make profiles every day, so it's important to ensure that OKC considers you active enough to keep featuring you highly in searches and feature you on the newsfeed on the main page. There are a few ways to do this.

Quickmatch Strategies

Quickmatch is a great tool for discovering women that would otherwise fall outside your search filters, and also makes you appear active on OKC. However, I think it is poorly used in most cases.

If you both rate each other 4-5 stars, then you are notified and matched. If you match, you *must* message her within 24 hours, lest you appear passive and even somewhat scared of messaging her. A woman will very rarely take the trouble to initiate a conversation with you because of how inundated they are with messages otherwise.

As I said before, Quickmatch is great for looking outside your filters – but the problem is that they don't provide their usernames to you. If you don't want to wait for her to potentially match you, simply type in key phrases verbatim from her profile into the OkCupid search function, find her, and take the offensive and message her!

Boosting Your Match Percentages

Some people view compatibility percentage as very important. I don't think they are necessarily indicative (and sometimes they are even wildly inaccurate), but it is unquestionable that when a woman sees your match percentage with her is over 90%, she gets curious about you.

So how do you game match questions? There are three simple steps.

First, take a minute and think about the type of woman you want to date. What is she like? What does she like? Is she active? Introverted? Artistic? Extroverted? Adventurous? And so on.

Second, answer 100 questions. Yes, really. It will take only 20 minutes. Answer them truthfully and with your target woman in mind, but stick to the strongest modifiers (Irrelevant, Very important, Mandatory) whenever possible. Match percentage rewards extremes, so using those modifiers will spike your match percentages with similar woman much more than the hedging modifiers inbetween. You will likely notice more match percentages over 90% and under 80% after this process.

Third, every day (yes!), answer 1-2 additional questions according to the timing noted below. This will cause OKC to treat you as an active user and show up higher in their search algorithms. The more active you are considered, the greater a chance you will show up on the newsfeed on the main page, which is amazing visibility.

I recommend staying away from the riskier questions related to sex and dating. Stay with safe, non-controversial questions because there are many potential red flags that could cause a woman to eject.

Photo Updates

Update your photos regularly. Same theory at work here – it makes OKC treat you as more active, and may entice women who like your new photo better than your old one.

Profile Updates

I know, you slaved over the right wording and spacing. But just re-word a few sentences throughout periodically. Same theory here.

Maximum visibility – what times of the day are optimal?

Think about it this way: what time would you make posts on Facebook to ensure the maximum number of likes and comments? You have to do it when people are most likely to be actively browsing the site. There are many arguments to be made here, but a general consensus has formed that people are most often browsing the Internet and various social media at the following time periods: 10am-12pm, 1pm-3pm, and 6pm-9pm.

Therefore, make the changes in this chapter during or before those time periods for maximum visibility and exposure.

What about instant messaging?

I would recommend not using this. There are a multitude of reasons why, but mostly it can only lead to you shooting yourself in the foot.

Chapter Nine: Messaging

In this chapter, we will learn how to craft unique messages that get replies, and how to transition those into equally exciting dates.

A General Overview

Sending a message is as easy as striking up a conversation in a bar, right? "Hey. Nice shoes. You come here much?"

Wait, no. Completely wrong. Your initial message to a woman is critical. It must conform to the **SURCCHH** system, be concise, and stand above the 20 other messages she might receive that day. In person, it might be relatively easy to convey that you both have a love of skiing and were born in Nebraska, but taking a similar straightforward approach online is as good as sending your message into a black hole. You might argue that being straightforward is the natural way to do it, but if there's something you should have taken away by this point of the book... there is a new "natural" for online dating that doesn't necessarily match up with real life.

Let's start with some hard guidelines before we dive deeper into message and conversation construction. Note the running theme of overvaluing the woman:

1. Humor is imperative.
2. No copy pastes.
3. Avoid asking too many questions like an interview. No more than 2 question marks in your initial message.
4. Don't compliment her physical appearance, and don't use more than 1 compliment, if any.
5. Do not comment on her looks.
6. Do not put her on a pedestal.

Countless female users have referred to the beginning of the week (Sunday and Monday) as "the flood." In other words, that's the time when most guys choose to message so they presumably have time to set up dates for the next weekend. You want to be the message that she opens first in her inbox, so message before the flood (Saturday afternoon) or after the flood (Tuesday night).

Six steps to an Amazing Message

Step one: Actually read her entire profile. No need to say the same about pictures, because you've already done so.

Step two: Note a few hooks she has that you can mention. Just like you do, women put hooks into their profile and pictures – openings for messages. The best hooks you use will be ones that you can relate to personally.

Step three: Think about how you can relate personally to those hooks, such as what your experiences, opinions, stories, and questions. Try to stay away from the most obvious hooks she uses (such as their usernames, or their red hair if they are a ginger) unless you have a truly kickass story, because she will get repeatedly messaged about those.

Step four: Create (1) a statement that begs a response that incorporates your personal relation to it, or (2) a question about the hook that incorporates your personal relation to it. Inject a humorous and lighthearted tone into your statement/question.

Step five: Create a statement that begs a response, or a question that relates to the *same* hook, or a *different* hook. This step is optional, and will be highly contextual. Sometimes you can send a message based on only one hook if you can relate strongly enough to it.

Step six: Combine and send. Don't explain why you messaged, don't be overly formal, and don't be wordy. Use correct grammar and spelling. Don't worry about signing it with your name yet. Don't even worry about starting the message with a salutation. Hit send and forget.

Keep in mind that the goal of your message isn't to introduce yourself and have her fall in love with you instantly, it's to get a positive reply. Act accordingly.

Examples with a Sample hottie

Let's examine a sample hottie you want to message so we can demonstrate exactly how those steps play out. We'll give her 10 hooks – though not all profiles are this hook-rich, she has a nice variety of common hooks that you'll find in many profiles. The examples will show exactly how I used hooks each time, made it personal to both of us, and made it stand out.

Another way of looking at it is to simply speak humorously about something you have in common. A final perspective is to make her laugh about something you both have knowledge about. These might sound repetitive, but I've learned that sometimes a fresh perspective of messaging a woman through online dating can help release the pressure of the ultimate goal of getting dates.

<u>All you're doing here is starting a conversation as organically as the medium will allow.</u>

Let's move on to our sample hottie.

Hottie says she:

1. Can be a homebody

2. Is a foodie

3. Is a nurse

4. Is from Idaho

5. Loves her dog named Ray

6. Wants to do a 10k soon

7. Loves country music

8. Has a picture in front of a waterfall

9. Has a picture playing the piano in a concert hall

10. Likes to play tennis

Examples

1. When I was 15, I shadowed my aunt (a nurse) into a childbirth, and knocked over a tray while almost fainting. You guys have nerves of steel.

What breed is Ray – let me guess, whippet?

2. My homebody phases usually pop up after going out a lot. I've taken it to mean that I'm actually an introvert that just does a decent job at acting like an extrovert.

How long ago did you move here from Idaho?

3. I love tennis, but my playing career peaked as an elementary school champion.

I just discovered Tim McGraw! Really trying to resist the temptation of buying cowboy boots...

4. Where was that piano concert? I recently bought a keyboard to get back into practice, but it doesn't work as well without my mother making me practice.

I just did my first 5K and am thinking about tackling the next level up!

5. Have you been to Trattoria Italy, the newly minted Michelin star restaurant? So worth it just for the lasagna.

That waterfall picture reminds me of a scene from "What Dreams May Come."

6. You'll never believe this, but last time I was in Idaho was for a tennis competition when I was 11. I remember it distinctly because that was the first time I tore my shorts when playing a match.

When did you move out here?

7. Are Florida Georgia Line and Hunter Hayes legit
   country, or am I just circling the entrance of the
   rabbit hole?

As a non-foodie, I know my last meal would be
something easy like steak and beer, what would yours
be?

8. Holy cow, when did you play in that concert hall?
   One of my dreams was always to play at Carnegie
   Hall, but then I hit 9th grade and suddenly soccer
   and girls became more important.

9. Doggie pro-tip: if Ray eats too fast and gets burpy,
   put a ball in his food dish to slow him down!

Find any hidden gems on Netflix lately?

10. That waterfall picture is amazing! Last time I went
    under one (in Mammoth) I could only stay for a

couple of minutes because it was so freezing. Where is that?

As you can see, funny anecdotes are the rule and not the exception, and staying playful is key. I constructed statements that will prompt her to reply, and introduced hooks of my own. It's really that simple.

The Exchange - what to do after the initial message

There are no hard and fast rules for the exchange of messages after your initial opener. Every exchange is inherently unique, so unfortunately I can't address every contingency. Just keep in mind that your overall goal is a date, and to move the conversation offline as quickly as possible. With that in mind:

1. **Do**: continue to use mini stories about new hooks and how they relate to both of you. This is difficult to define, but abide by **SURCCHH** and keep it simple.

2. **Do**: include a couple of questions or statements that beg her to answer in each message.

3. **Do**: refer to local locations, events, and activities. These can easily be referred to later when transitioning to a date. Take some time and

research some interesting events, date ideas, and locations, especially new and hip ones.

4. **Do**: use a balance of humor and sincerity.

5. **Don't**: be overly aggressive or use sexual innuendos.

6. **Don't**: reply at odd hours of the night. It carries weird connotations.

7. **Don't**: drive the conversation towards negative or overly serious subjects.

8. **Don't**: debate her, but don't defer to her opinions either.

9. **Don't**: write novels. You might feel compelled to reciprocate if her message to you is long, but take that sign of interest from her and transition to a date early rather than over-writing.

10. **Don't**: let the conversation turn into an interview, and stay away from the typical "who, what, where, when, why" questions.

Transitioning to a date ideally takes 3-6 messages... and shouldn't take more. You'll have to judge when to ask her out based on how comfortable and interested in you she seems. Look for the length of her replies, if she's bantering back at you and asking questions, and how long she takes to reply.

If you're ever in doubt of whether to ask her out, the best thing you can do... is simply ask her out. No one joins online dating sites for pen pals.

-"Is she actually interested?" Ask her out to find out.

-"She doesn't seem interested, though." Ask her out and find out.

-"She didn't pick up on my hint of asking her out." Ask her out, that's a strong hint. And so on.

The Transition – messaging your way to the date

Transitioning into a date can be very natural. This is the main way I recommend, though there are many methods.

1. Reply and react to something she said in her most recent message to you.

2. At the end of the message, refer to the activity/event/location seed you planted. If you didn't plant one, simply introduce an activity/event/location that you've researched.

3. Set a specific time and place, and ask if she is available.

4. Sign it with your name.

If you've made it to message 3 with a woman, chances are that the date is now yours to lose. She is already interested and is just waiting for you to make that move.

Example:

Yeah, I think John Mayer is a little overrated as well, but that doesn't stop me from buying his new albums in the hopes that he makes a comeback to more acoustic sounds. Was he the last person you saw live?

I've been meaning to check out that new bar, Harry's. Do you want to check it out this Thursday, say 730pm?

-Mario

If she accepts your invitation, here's your reply:

I know, I can't believe they have a freakin' piñata there on Sundays either. My number is xxx-xxx-xxxx in case we need to talk before then.

See you there!

Don't worry about getting her phone number just then. Chances are that she'll reply with it. If she does, you should be sure to shoot a confirmation/reminder text on the day of the date, if it's more than a few days away.

What if she goes cold?

It's entirely common for women to go cold. That is, you are having an engaging conversation with a woman, and she simply stops replying. So what do you do then? *Note: this does not apply to initial messages to women. If they don't reply to those, it is very likely they simply are not interested.*

There are only two things you can do: wait, or send a second message. I recommend the first, then the second.

Depending on the nature and engagement of your conversation, wait somewhere from 3-5 days to see if see if she actually replies, then send a *short* follow-up after that cut-off point. If she's not interested anymore, is seeing another guy exclusively now, is out of town, or any other reason, she simply won't reply. (It's important to repeat that most potential reasons probably aren't even related to you.) If she is still interested and was working things out with any number of issues in her life, then she'll be glad to see your message. The second message is literally a no-lose situation.

Make sure that your tone is nonchalant, or else it will probably be perceived as desperate. You can go two ways: either just a statement, or just directly asking her out. The following example combines both.

Example: *(referring to something from the most previous message you sent, and how you came upon it nonchalantly)* You know, I just stumbled upon a John Mayer Pandora station today, and I think his more recent albums do keep that older vibe.

I know we were talking about that place Harry's, but my friend just told me about a place that's even crazier, Winston's. I'm free this Thursday at 7, care to check it out?

What if she cancels or postpones the date?

As with not replying and going cold, there are a multitude of reasons why this could have happened. How should you handle her cancelling or postponing without suggesting another time? (If she immediately suggests another time, don't worry. You're probably still in.)

You must project a dominant mindset. You are an eligible, attractive man with many potential options and plans, and her cancellation or postponement does not affect your mood. Remember, regardless of whether you actually possess this mindset, you must *project* it. Do *not* show disappointment or desperation.

So if she texts/emails/messages a variation of "I'm so sorry, I have a family dinner and I can't make it to XMI Bar, so raincheck," your reply should be strong and maintain control of the interaction. Don't dwell on the canceled date, and move the conversation along.

Step 1: If she gives you any detail about the reason she cancels, make some quick conversation about it. For example, "No problem, big family get-together?" If she doesn't give you any detail, go immediately to Step 2.

Step 2: After she replies, eject from the conversation. For example, "Cool, some other time then."

Step 3: Depending on the chemistry and vibe you've gotten from her, wait somewhere from 3-5 days to re-establish contact. For example, "Hey! How's your schedule on Thursday? Let's check out Oscar's."

Step 4: What if she doesn't reply within a reasonable amount of time? For example, you re-establish contact on Monday, ask her out for Thursday, and she still hasn't replied on Thursday morning? How does a dominant mindset deal with this? You have two choices: you can either accept it as a sign of rejection and let it go, or shoot a short text. For example, "Didn't hear back from you so I let my friends convince me to go line dancing! Next time." She will either ignore it, or reply with an apology because you've subtly called her out on being a flake. Either way, you'll find out where you stand with her.

Chapter Ten: General Tips

In this chapter, we'll run through a few general pieces of advice to maximize your experience as whole.

Date Segmentation and Logistics

After you've got your date scheduled, you need to think about how to create a date she'll want to gush to her friends about... if you end up liking her. Plan the date in *segments* with natural ending points, which will allow you to bail early if you so wish, and also make you appear fun and spontaneous. For example, if you almost fell asleep during your first activity with her, your natural ending point is when that activity ends. You can both go your separate ways, and you save your time and money.

But if you like her and the feeling is mutual, then you can go proceed with the subsequent segment in your logistics plan, which you have arranged before the date.

This is an easy process. You've clearly already set up an activity that she agreed to, so now it's time to do a little bit of support research. Before you go on your date, make sure you have the following easily accessible in your head:

1. What are 2 nearby *venues* you can go to after the initial date activity? *Bar, tapas restaurant, lounge, your place, a park with swings, a scenic view, etc.*

2. What are 2 nearby actual *activities* you can do after the initial date activity? *Karaoke, a walk/stroll, scenic view with a bottle of wine, billiards, bowling, biking, etc.*

If the first segment went well, proceed to the next. And so on. For an optimal date, I would recommend trying to complete 3 segments total. It keeps things moving, helps conversation, makes you seem knowledgeable and spontaneous, and creates more opportunity for flirting. It's also a great barometer into how she feels about you – if she keeps agreeing to go onto your next date segment, it's usually a very telling sign. Other things to plan for:

3. Proximity to public transport and your apartment?

4. How familiar are you with the area? Get familiar!

5. Are you likely to run into people you know while out? In most cases, this is a plus.

6. Do you know the owners of any establishments? This is a major plus.

7. Can you showcase any skills or talents during any of the activities? For example, if you can sing, subtly suggest karaoke.

Simple Texting Guidelines

This could be an entire book by itself, so here are the two things I have to say on the matter. First, no one ever regrets *not* sending that last text. It feels empowering to have the last word in a conversation and decide when it ends, as opposed to half-heartedly waiting on a response. Second, don't send texts that don't depend on a response from her.

Using Your Week Wisely

From your initial message, you should make it a goal to have a date set up within the following week, or the next week at latest. You must strike while the iron is hot.

For first dates with women, I would shoot for a weekday evening, or weekend afternoon affair. These are lower investment times that will allow you to utilize your date segments effectively.

Thursday, Friday, and Saturday nights are prime real estate, so they should be reserved for dates with women you are in more advanced stages with.

Invisible Browsing and Saving Profiles

I highly encourage not browsing invisibly. If you visit someone, it greatly increases the chance that they visit your profile, which is more than you might get if you just sent them a message. And of course, you can see whoever was intrigued enough by your picture to view you, so you know who might better receive a message from you. There are no downsides... unless you're a compulsive clicker.

Not enabling invisible browsing shows the other user exactly what time you last visited them. The first time is fine, and serves the purpose of exposure and visibility. The second time might also be fine... but it really goes downhill after that if you keep viewing them every time you send them a message, get curious about them, or in general just click too much.

To avoid appearing needy, too interested, too eager, like you're checking if she's on, or like a stalker, after a woman has replied to you, feel free to view her profile again... to save the page as a PDF so you don't have to refer to it again.

If you feel compelled to check for the last time that she was online, try to refrain. It's never an accurate indicator of their actual activity on the site, and will just serve to drive you insane.

Concluding Remarks

You probably won't even be reading this chapter because you'll be busy exchanging messages with attractive women.

But...

It is my sincere hope that no matter your level of experience with online dating, you've found something worthwhile in this book. The beauty of the **SURCCHH** system is that it's applicable to everyone and extends out of the dating realm – I've often received feedback of boosted and revitalized self-esteem when clients were able to think outside the box to discover what makes them unique and great.

If you've followed my principles, you will truly have succeeded in the goals I proposed at the beginning of the book. You are now armed to the teeth to take your online dating to the next level.

Now get back to crafting that **SURCCHH** system-approved message and happy dating!

Sincerely,

Patrick King

Dating and Image Coach

www.PatrickKingConsulting.com

P.S. If you enjoyed this book, please don't be shy and drop me a line, leave a review, or both! I love reading feedback, and reviews are the lifeblood of Kindle books, so they are always welcome and greatly appreciated.

Other books by Patrick King include:

The Online Dating Bible: 33 Proven Commandments to Create a Stunning Profile, Write Alluring Messages, and Get All the Dates You Can Handle
http://www.amazon.com/dp/B00Q0ZSEDO

Charm Her Socks Off: Creating Chemistry from Thin
Air http://www.amazon.com/dp/B00IEO688W

CHATTER: Small Talk, Charisma, and How to Talk to
Anyone http://www.amazon.com/dp/B00J5HH2Y6

22980143R00065

Made in the USA
San Bernardino, CA
01 August 2015